ON THE
OTHER SIDE OF THE
PULPIT
"God is Still Real"

ON THE OTHER SIDE OF THE
PULPIT

"God is Still Real"

Portraits of the life of
Dr. Dallas F. Billington

Witnessed by S. *Neal Kendall*

XULON PRESS

Xulon Press
2301 Lucien Way #415
Maitland, FL 32751
407.339.4217
www.xulonpress.com

Unless otherwise indicated, Scripture quotations taken from the
King James Version (KJV) – *public domain.*

Printed in the United States of America

Paperback ISBN-13: 978-1-6628-0568-4
Ebook ISBN-13: 978-1-6628-0569-1

FOREWORD

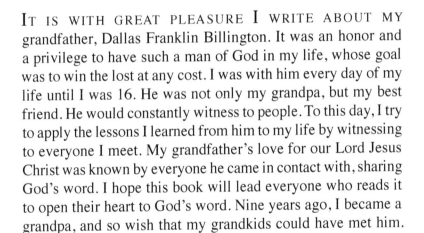

It is with great pleasure I write about my grandfather, Dallas Franklin Billington. It was an honor and a privilege to have such a man of God in my life, whose goal was to win the lost at any cost. I was with him every day of my life until I was 16. He was not only my grandpa, but my best friend. He would constantly witness to people. To this day, I try to apply the lessons I learned from him to my life by witnessing to everyone I meet. My grandfather's love for our Lord Jesus Christ was known by everyone he came in contact with, sharing God's word. I hope this book will lead everyone who reads it to open their heart to God's word. Nine years ago, I became a grandpa, and so wish that my grandkids could have met him. My prayer is to be like Grandpa, to live my life so close to God that my kids and grandkids can see Christ living in me.

Charles Franklin Billington Jr.

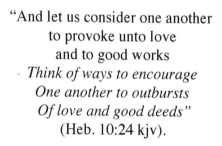

"And let us consider one another
to provoke unto love
and to good works
Think of ways to encourage
One another to outbursts
Of love and good deeds"
(Heb. 10:24 kjv).

PREFACE

I WROTE THIS BOOK TO ACKNOWLEDGE, HONOR, AND thank Dr. Dallas F. Billington for his unwavering service to Jesus Christ. He was a man who always gave all glory to God for his accomplishments. Preacher, as he was best known, said he found early in life that success did not come from what he did but that which came from the hands God. God can give breath, success, strength, health, wisdom, talents, gifts, and life, but God will not give glory for all glory belongs to Him. *"I am the Lord: that is my name: and my glory will I not give to another, neither My praise to graven images"* (Isa. 42:8).

Dr. Dallas F. Billington was born near the small town of Kirksey, Kentucky in 1903. He left home when he was seventeen to work at the International Shoe Factory in Paducah, Kentucky. The talk was that there were good paying jobs in Akron, Ohio. In February 1925 he moved from Paducah, Kentucky to Akron, Ohio and immediately obtained work at the Goodyear Tire & Rubber Company to build tires. He always said God did not call him to Akron to build tires but to build a church. And he did.

He founded the Akron Baptist Temple in 1935. He orchestrated its growth from eighty original members to what a leading

Christian research organization called "the home of the world's largest Sunday school." He died August 1972

Preacher's most important task in life was to win lost souls.

I write this book as a testament for others, to show them how God can use a person who goes all out for Christ.

We may not possess a doctor or reverend title in front of our names, or may never have attended a Bible school, but we can still be encouragers. Nowhere in the Bible does it speak of a part-time Christian. If you are born again, you are a full-time Christian, whether you are on a church staff or you build tires.

> *"And let us consider how we may spur one another on toward love and good deeds, not giving up meeting together, as some are in the habit of doing, but encouraging one another — and all the more as you see the day approaching"* *(Heb. 10:24-25).*

The verse above does not say to meet to hear the preacher or sing along, but to encourage one another. God knows the importance of one-on-one interaction. It is easy to believe what God did in certain situations—He is God. However, to hear how another human filled with the Holy Spirit reacts to trials, sorrows and tribulations reinforces our belief and faith and establish hope that what God did for others he can do for us.

A little boy once said, "Mom, would you help me put on my shirt?" Mom said, "Johnny, you know how to put on your shirt; you have done it many times." Johnny replied, "Yeah, Mom, but it feels so good to have a little help."

It is my prayer that after reading this book others who have been born again by the grace of God may see the purpose of their Christian life—to be Christlike and encourage others to see how their life can be an inspiration.

A song I wrote entitled, "He Walked With God," says:

> *Someone's watching the steps you take,*
> *They see the things you do and your mistakes,*
> *They see the life you live, and they hear your talk,*
> *From these things, they can tell if with God you walk.*

There are times we all feel like our lives do not matter, that what we say, what we do, and how we act, make no difference. We fail to realize others are judging our actions. Many think God saves us so we can go to Heaven, but God says in John 15:16, *"Ye have not chosen me, but I have chosen you, and ordained you, that ye should go and bring forth fruit."* We become His hands, feet, and lips to spread His word. By the same token, Satan can do nothing without a body. That is why Satan wants you, why he continually jostles and condemns you. We must learn to say, *"Get thee behind me, Satan"* (Matt. 16:23).

You may have heard the story of the young man who went to a lumber camp in the Northwest for a summer job. His mother thought of these men as hard individuals, and with much concern asked her son when he returned how he had sustained his Christian faith. The young man said, "I just never told them."

My prayer is that whether you are a young babe in Christ or have been a Christian for many years, that this book will instill in you the importance of 2 Timothy 4:2, *"Preach the word, be instant in season, out of season, with all long suffering and reprove, rebuke, exhort with all long suffering and doctrine."*

Furthermore, if you have never asked forgiveness for your sins, you need Jesus. Will you accept Him today?

S. Neal Kendall
July 29, 2020

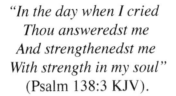

*"In the day when I cried
Thou answeredst me
And strengthenedst me
With strength in my soul"*
(Psalm 138:3 KJV).

INTRODUCTION

FOR A LONG TIME, I PONDERED WRITING A BOOK about my church pastor, Dr. Dallas F. Billington. However, with work, and the daily frenzy life, I decided to wait for retirement. Now that day has come. But I now understand the comic Abner Dean when he entitled his book, "What am I doing here?" To be honest, it seemed like an impossible task.

To fully understand the relevance of this book, I must tell you how I grew up. It will help to explain why one person had such an impact on my life and why I felt the need to tell others about him.

"You are not to play with that Kendall kid; he's up to no good." This is what other mothers told their children. They considered me to be from the other side of the tracks. Then as now, if your poor, you are considered a bad influence.

I grew up with nothing. I was born and spent most of my early life in Copley, Ohio. I remember my mother would wash and iron my shirt and pants as soon as I got home from school so I could wear them again the next day. This would go on until a neighbor or organization furnished us with some used clothes.

My dad made reasonable wages as a truck driver for a cement company but spent most of it on alcohol. In those days, people who drank too much were not called alcoholics—he was the town drunk. I was well known by the town constable, who called almost every Saturday night to tell me which bar in his township he was at. My job was to pick him up—literally—and carry him home. He would be in a stupor, not knowing where he was.

Almost every day after work, he stopped to have a few before coming home. Some people get silly when they drink. My dad got belligerent. Therefore, my early home life was like a war zone. There was an angry man in the house who spent more time away than at home, which in a way was better. I never knew what it was like to have a genuine father.

Although I earned achievements in sports and other school activities, I never had a relative to watch me play or perform. After a game, my friend's relatives gathered around them with congratulations and hugs. I walked or hitch-hiked home in the dark.

One morning before school, I woke up to find Dad sitting in a chair at the end of my bed with a shotgun in his lap, pointed at me. God allowed him to fall into a stupor, or that might have been the end of the story. I picked up the gun and removed the shells and hid them under the matrices. I then placed the gun back in his lap, got dressed and went to school

When I think of my days of youth, I remember humiliations. When I was around nine years old, a school friend who was a Boy Scout invited me to go with him to summer camp for a week. On the first morning at camp, the leader inspected how we had made our beds. He reprimanded me in a loud voice for not placing my folded pajamas under my pillow. I did not know what pajamas were, as I had never owned any.

At the end of the week, we packed our bags and walked across a field to the parking lot where the parents waited. My friend's dad picked him up in his arms and hugged him and gave him a kiss on the check. I had seen nothing like that before, such fatherly affection and love.

My mother endured years of conflict, aggression, and hostilities. She still made sure we were in church every Sunday morning. When I was fourteen years old, attending the small church near our home, I knelt and ask God to forgive me of all my sins.

As my faith grew, I came to realize with God I had found the Father I never had before.

I graduated from high school when I was sixteen. Within two weeks, I got a job, found an apartment, and left home.

I started playing guitar and singing in high school. This was before country western style—back then it was called hillbilly music. I continued singing after graduation and ended up performing in several bars and shady places in Akron, Ohio. I was too young to be allowed in these spots but I guess since I was entertaining it was okay. I played sometimes with a back-up band and sometimes solo.

At one of these places where I performed solo, a guy who played a mean electric guitar would often join me in the background. One night, he told me he had booked engagements in Pennsylvania and New York. He said, "I can't sing a lick, but I think the two of us could really do it up." I was to call him Monday morning to let him know my decision.

On Sunday night I found myself in the little church where I was saved, listening to a quartet of black singers/musicians. When the bass sang, you could almost feel the chairs shake, and when the high tenor sang, you felt he could shatter a crystal glass. I had never heard such harmony in all my life. On the way home I felt as if God said, "Now *that* is what I want you to do." Monday morning, I called the guitarist and told him thanks, but God asked me to sing gospel.

If you are wondering what happened to that guy, he went on to become the famous well-known musician-Chet Atkins.

I saw in the paper that the Blackwood Brothers Quartet was singing at the Akron Baptist Temple. The music drew me there. The name Dallas Billington never rang a bell.

I began attending Akron Baptist Temple regularly. Soon, Bob Johnson, Chuck Ramsey, Clint Hall, and I formed The Temple Aires Quartet. We practiced three nights a week and performed Saturday and sometimes three times on Sunday . The choir directors scheduled me to sing solos before the message.

The route between auditoriums led through the main office. One Sunday morning while passing through, Dallas (aka preacher) called me into his office. He said, "When you sing people sit up and notice. You project the words of the song and they want to hear it. I want you to become apart of our music program and go with me when I hold services in other places. All I ask is that you keep your nose clean. I can't have you singing gospel at church and courting Satan at the same time. I'm not going to follow you around. That's between you and God and if you want to tick God off, don't say I didn't warn you."

Salvation changed my life. As a new convert, sometimes I wondered about the dubious actions and talk of some who claimed to be saved. Preacher's admonition to, "keep my nose clean," rang loud and clear.

We were going through an era of "two-faced" individuals, not only those in the pew but prominent religious figures, as well: Jim Jones and his Kool-Aid, Jim and Tammy Baker TV evangelists, Jimmy Swaggart's questionable activities, and Rex Humbard and his girdle factory, to name a few.

I told Dr. Dallas and his son Dr. Charles several times how exhilarating it was to go to work and not have to explain any of my pastor's extracurricular activities. I had firsthand knowledge regarding the out-of-pulpit talk and actions of other ministers compared to Dallas. Not only was I used in the church services in Akron, I also traveled many miles with Preacher to participate in dedications and evangelistic services at our satellite churches—the Mansfield Baptist Temple, Canton Baptist Temple, Toledo Baptist Temple, Cleveland Baptist Church, Youngstown Baptist Temple, Warren Baptist Temple, as well as senior citizen centers and pastoral conventions.

I never understood why he took this snotty-nosed kid to sing the solos and lead the music when the church had so many other talented musicians.

Since I never had a father to learn from, those miles were consumed with my continual questions directed at the Pastor. Years later, I realized what a privileged, eye-opening experience God had allowed me to receive and enjoy in my theological education.

The purpose of this book—*On the Other Side of the Pulpit*—is to emphasize that it is possible for a person filled with the Holy Spirit to resist Satan and the worlds way.

To react the same in season and out of season, to adhere to the words of Jesus who said, *"If I be lifted up from the earth, will draw all men unto me."* (John 12:32) Dr. Dallas Billington's desire and aim in life, whether behind the pulpit preaching a sermon, pumping gas, getting a haircut, or eating at a restaurant, was to "Win the lost at any cost."

Most Chapters begin with a question I asked preacher.

Next came his answer.

Followed by my interpretation and comments on the subject.

Part 1

QUESTIONS

Chapter 1

BE CALM

———— ⌒⌒⌒ ————

"Preacher, what is the secret to remaining calm while performing in front of people?"

We stood at the back of the funeral home, waiting a few minutes for our time to walk to the front and begin the service. I would open the service with a solo. Being an introvert, I had an uneasy feeling in my stomach and began to sweat. Preacher held his Bible in one hand and appeared calm as a cucumber.

He turned, put his Bible under one arm and held out both open hands. His palms looked like he had held them under a spigot and not dried them. "Everyone is different," he said. "For me, it's sweating hands. God called me to preach. He will give me the words. So, I don't think about my performance or mistakes. My hands sweat because it's the thought that what I say or don't say may be the difference of where someone spends eternity."

Our conversation recalled the old song, "You're the only Jesus some will ever see." Preacher lived his life to keep people out of hell. I walked to the podium and looked over the congregation as the interlude was playing wondering if all of them would make Heaven their home.

I sang "If We Never Meet Again This Side of Heaven." Then Preacher spoke, repeating many of the phrases from the song and saying if there was anyone present who had not asked forgiveness of their sins, they would never see the one in the casket again. He said this because he knew the deceased to be born again.

It was always encouraging to have the preacher weave your song into his message.

Since then when there are times I stand before an audience with apprehension God reminds me of Isaiah 41:10, *Fear thou not, for I am with thee :be not dismayed, for I am thy God: I will strengthen thee; yea, I will help thee; yea I will uphold thee with the right hand of my righteousness.*

Chapter 2

MAKE THEM MAD

"WHAT ARE YOU GOING TO SING FOR ME TONIGHT?"
Preacher asked me.

We were headed to southern Ohio for a rally. Dr. Charles
Billington, preacher's son, was driving. It was a running joke
with those who ever rode with Charles driving that you got
closer to the Lord and brushed up on your prayer life. He followed in his dad's footsteps of preaching the word of God
without comprise. Charles was considered an excellent Pilot and
often when he held meetings, would fly there with our quartet.

Dallas was in the passenger seat and Clyde White (piano player)
and I in the back seat. When asked, I told him the songs I had
in mind but offered to sing whatever he felt most appropriate.

Preacher turned halfway around with his arm on the top of the
front seat. He said, "Well, if you can, how about singing the
one that says something like, *Souls are crying, men are dying,
won't you lead them to the cross?* 'Cause I am going to make
them mad tonight. If I can make them mad, they will sit up and
listen to every word I say, hoping to hear more so they have

more reason to punch me in the nose. Then I have their attention, and I can stop and tell them about Jesus You can be the best orator alive with the best sermon ever preached, but if the audience is asleep or thinking about what they're going to eat afterwards, you might as well close your Bible and go home."

I said, "Oh yeah, we can do that. The song goes this way." And I sang it for them, "Souls are crying, men are dying, won't you lead them to the cross? Go and find them, help to win them, win the lost at any cost."

When you think about it, Jesus used objects to get peoples attention. Like setting the little boy on his lap to tell them they must become as a little child. Preacher would tell present day stories to get the listeners attention.

One true story from the newspaper that he used more than once, was of two men who raped a girl and killed her. With the help of bloodhounds, they were able to find the evil men. He pointed out that if someone who commits murder cannot get away from a dog, how do you expect to get away from God with the sins you have committed.

Chapter 3

COSMETICS

"PREACHER, WHAT DO YOU THINK ABOUT ALL THIS talk concerning women's use of makeup?"

Years ago, this was a hot topic in many churches. Some either forbid their women members from wearing any makeup, or they were very vocal about their opinion whether you wanted to hear it or not. These individuals believed it was a sin to paint your face. This included some Baptist churches.

Preacher responded by saying, "I'll tell you something—I believe that an old barn always looks better with a fresh coat of paint. Man is made of body, soul, and spirit. The important thing is, do you have a pretty mind, do you have a pretty heart, do you have a pretty soul? 1 Peter 3:3 says, '*Your beauty should not come from outward adornment. The question should be, what is your motive? God looks at the heart.*'"

Chapter 4

ACADEMIC DEGREES

"Preacher, how does it feel to have earned a doctoral degree. Do you feel people will think you're smarter now and listen more closely?"

"I have never thought much about obtaining a higher education," Preacher said. "My desire is to spend my time being taught by God on the important things. Education is important, but does it make you smarter? No. More knowledgeable, yes; more intelligent, no.

"I have always heard it said that no matter how many curly cues are on the end of a pig's tail, it is still just a pig."

> "The fear of the Lord is the beginning of knowledge; fools despise wisdom and instruction" (Prov. 1:7).

> "For the Lord gives wisdom, from his mouth come knowledge and understanding" (Prov. 2:6).

Preachers work experience building tires allowed him to understand how the average person, saved or unsaved, thought and felt. This gave him the ability to talk and preach on their level. People did not feel he was talking down to them or that he, as a preacher, thought he was better than they.

A good illustration is when Jesus the King of Kings, and Lord of Lords, who flung this universe into space, proved this when He lay down his life on the cross for our sins. And who can forget when Jesus took off His robe, wrapped a towel around his waist, poured water into a basin, and washed the feet of his disciples, then dried them with the towel in John 13:1-17.

I saw this plaque hanging in Cracker Barrels restaurant. Remember this food for thought, if you remember nothing else: "You cannot look down your nose at someone else while you are washing their feet."

Chapter 5

KNEE KNOCKING

"PREACHER, WHY IS IT WHEN I STAND BEHIND THAT microphone my knees feel like they're knocking together louder than the music?"

We were at the WAKR television studio on Copley Road in Akron, Ohio. Our foray into television production was in its infancy. The format for each segment was to have songs by a soloist, duet, or quartet and then a message from one of the four ministers.

One portrait of life occurred when I was scheduled for a solo. Just before leaving home for the studio, I received a phone call from the choir director. He related to me that all the ministers were in Columbus, Ohio for a united meeting and forgot to plan for the speaker that night. It was a little nerve wracking to do the whole telecast single-handed on a 30-minute notice.

The next step was to move the cameras into the church and pro-duce the entire Sunday morning service. All services where live at this time and were not taped or edited of mistakes.

When I asked the preacher about my nerves he was sitting behind a desk while I sat on the edge, half-on and half-off. The desk was a prop. We never used it for the broadcast, just to rest before the light signaled the start of the show.

He said, "Well, let me tell you something. The day you can stand behind the microphone and lift your head in song like you are standing in the shower at home, hitting all those high notes and singing like a bird with no effort, will be the day you have lost your effectiveness for the Lord. For what you will be saying is, 'I can do this on my own and I don't need any help.'"

"You will find you cannot do it on your own. In God's work, you need the Holy Spirit to take those words and plant them in the listener's heart to make them realize they need Jesus."

"The Lord is my strength and my song. HE is become my salvation" (Exod. 15:2KJV).

It has been fifty years since then. I have sung in many quartets and solo performances in the United States and Europe. I always talk to God before picking up the mic.

I'm reminded of a sign on a billboard, "I want to be so full of the Holy Spirit, that if a mosquito bites me, it will fly away singing, "There's Power in The Blood."

If I had some words of wisdom for babes in Christ, singing God's word, they would be, whatever time you take practicing the song you plan to sing, take the same time talking to Jesus about the song. Don't be surprised if he has you change the song.

I remember handing the sound engineer a music CD to play for the song I was using for the morning service. I almost lost it when I realized it was not the song I had practiced. In my haste getting out of the car, I had picked up the wrong CD. I headed to the car, then stopped and thought, Maybe it's not the wrong song.

It was a song I had not sang for a long time. I prayed God would help me remember the words. After the service, two people stopped me to say how much that song meant to them.

I seem to make a lot of mistakes, but God never does.

Chapter 6

ILLITERACY

"PREACHER, HOW DO YOU HANDLE IT WHEN SO MANY people ask you to pray for them?"

"Well, let me explain something," Preacher answered me. "There are those in deep sorrow, as in the death of a loved one, for example, who ask me to pray with them. I will drop everything and pray with them. There are others who ask me to pray on behalf of them for something they feel they need.

"For some, I will tell them about the man who asked his pastor to pray for him. A week later, the man asked the pastor if he had prayed for him. The pastor said, 'I did.' 'Well,' the man asked, 'what did He say?' The pastor said, 'God said why doesn't he ask me himself.' Prayer is personal and God may want to get his attention."

If we are born-again believers in Jesus Christ, we are in the same boat. Some believers have been saved for years yet are still, as Jesus says, babes living on milk instead of growing in faith. If you want to talk to Jesus, pray. If you want Jesus to talk to you, read His word. This is the way to grow and become strong Christians so you can teach others.

David did not need to know Goliath's strength; he already knew the strength of God.

There are 340 million people in the USA. Seventy percent say they are Christians. That means 238 million Christians live in American. If that many people were living the Christlike life, this would be Heaven on earth.

Let us see what statistics offer. Will Mancini, who operates a church consulting firm, finds a disturbing trend. He says, especially in the last few years, one common thread has become a common rope. Every church he talks with, regardless of denomination or size, reports that their members attend worship service less frequently than ever. For example, people who used to attend four times a month may now only attend three. Members who used to come twice a month will only come once a month, and so on.

The consequence is, we will not believe more than we know, and we will not live higher than our beliefs. If you only go as far as History 101, your beliefs cannot go any further until you continue with History 102.

We must give urgent attention to a serious problem—biblical illiteracy in the church. This scandalous problem is our own, and it is up to us to fix it. Researchers George Gallup and Jim Castelli write: "Americans revere the Bible but, by and large, they don't read it. And because they do not read it, they have become a nation of biblical illiterates."

How bad is it? Researchers tell us it is worse than most could imagine. Fewer than half of all adults can name the four gospels.

Many Christians cannot identify more than two or three of the disciples. Sixty percent of Americans cannot name even five of the Ten Commandments.

"No wonder people break the Ten Commandments all the time. They do not know what they are. Increasingly, America has become biblically illiterate." said George Barna, president of The Barna Group"

Multiple surveys reveal the problem in stark terms. Eighty-two percent of Americans believe "God helps those who help themselves" is a Bible verse. Those identified as born-again Christians did better by only one percent. Most adults think the Bible teaches that the most important purpose in life is taking care of one's family.

Some statistics are enough to perplex even those aware of the problem. A Barna poll showed that at least twelve percent of adults believe that Joan of Arc was Noah's wife. Another survey of graduating high school seniors revealed that over fifty percent thought Sodom and Gomorrah were husband and wife. A considerable number of respondents to one poll indicated that Billy Graham preached the Sermon on the Mount.

In 2008, a certain political party voted to throw God out of their platform. Americans increasingly live in a scripture-free public space. The larger scandal is biblical ignorance among Christians. Choose whichever statistic or survey you like; the general pattern is the same. They show that America's Christians know less and less about the Bible. How can a generation be biblically shaped in its understanding of human sexuality when it believes Sodom and Gomorrah to be a married couple?

No wonder Christians show a growing tendency to compromise on the issue of homosexuality. Many who identify themselves as Christians are similarly confused about the gospel itself. For they go along with and vote for those who murder little babies in the mother's womb at the tune of 3,000 a day. An individual who believes that "God helps those who help themselves" will find salvation by grace and justification by faith to be alien concepts.

This really is our problem, and it is up to this silent generation of Christians to reverse course.

We will not believe more than we know, and we will not live higher than our beliefs. We can trace the many fronts of Christian compromise in this generation to biblical illiteracy in the pews and the absence of biblical preaching and teaching in our homes and churches. This generation must get deadly serious about the problem of biblical illiteracy, or a frighteningly large number of Americans—Christians included— will go on thinking that Sodom and Gomorrah lived happily ever after.

We need to understand that the problems of our country are not in the White House. The problems of our country are not in the courthouse. The problems of our country are not in the schoolhouse. The problems of our country are in the church house.

Christians need to stand on the promises instead of sitting on the premises. We need to tell the world, right from wrong, according to God's word. I am afraid too many are "putting their light under a bushel."

"We cannot afford to let down our Christian standards just to hold the interest of people who want to go to hell and still belong to a church" (A. W. Tozer).

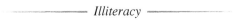
"I believe that one reason why the church, at this present moment, has so little influence over the world is because the world has so much influence over the church" (Charles Haddon Spurgeon).

Chapter 7

TRULY A CHRISTIAN

"PREACHER, I GREW UP IN A DYSFUNCTIONAL HOME. You speak of your father and mother as being devout Christians. You tell how you went to church many years before accepting the Lord. So, how did you know you were truly saved?"

"For me it became quite evident," he said. "Before being saved, I never ran from a fight. After salvation, I was working my shift at the Goodyear Tire and Rubber company when a violent situation occurred. There was a lot of name-calling, and we were ready for fisticuffs. I had a heavy metal weight in my hand. One blow with that object could have possibly killed a man.

"Before being saved, I would have fought bitterly. But things were different. It never crossed my mind to strike him. God had changed my heart; He changed my mind; He changed my thinking. God had replaced it with a heart of love and taught me to forgive and to control my fists. Those many days in the rubber plant taught me many lessons. Now, I had only one desire in life and that was to see people saved."

A father asked his four-year-old why he would not do as he was told. The boy said, "Daddy, I just don't want to." Many of us Christians are not that honest. We make excuses for not obeying God's will when the real reason is, we just do not want to. You have heard people ask certain Christians why they are not allowed to do anything. And some Christians when asked to go places or take part in certain activities will say, "I'm not allowed to do that," Or some will even feel sorry for themselves and say, "I can't have any fun at all because I can't do anything, as a Christian."

You have heard hecklers say, "You Christians feel you have a crutch. You can do anything you want, then ask for forgiveness and go out and do the same things."

I want you to know that, as a Christian, I can do anything I want. I can go anyplace I want. I can say anything I want; I can drink and eat anything I want. Why? Because John 8:36 says, "If the Son therefore shall make you free, ye shall be free indeed." The Greek word for free indeed is ON-Tice El-yoo-ther-us, meaning unrestrained (to go at pleasure as a citizen, verily of a truth, of a certainty).

Therefore, as a Christian, I can do anything I want. The difference is, as a born-again believer in the Lord Jesus Christ who washed my sins away at Calvary, I became a child of GOD, and my want to has changed. I no longer desire or want to do anything that would displease God.

> *"Therefore, if any man be in Christ, he is a new creature: old things are passed away; behold, all things are become new"* (2 Cor 5:17).

The answer to this dilemma is in 1 John 5:3. *"For this is the love of God, that we keep his commandments: and his commandments are not grievous."*

Our love for GOD and what He did for us makes doing his will more desirable than doing our will. I can do anything I want to do, but my want to has changed, so I don't want to go to places I feel my LORD would not want me to be. I don't want to say things that would grieve the LORD. Is there something you know is GOD'S will for you? Do you love HIM enough to desire it and do it? Christ did not want to go to the Cross if there was another way. "And He went a little farther, and fell on his face, and prayed, saying, *O my Father, if it be possible, let this cup pass from me: nevertheless not as I will, but as thou wilt"* (Matt. 26:39). Christ didn't take the easy road because He wanted to do the will of His Father. *"Thinkest thou that I cannot now pray to my Father, he shall presently give me more than twelve legions of angels? But how then shall the scriptures be fulfilled, that thus it must be?"* (Matt. 26:53-54).

Putting your faith in Jesus is life's most important decision.

Faith in Christ is not a onetime choice but a lifetime challenge.

Do you remember asking Christ into your heart? If you are a true Christian, you will want to please the Father and do as His will. Dear Lord, I know you died on the cross for my sins. I recognize I am a sinner. I ask forgiveness of all my sins and to be saved for Christ's sake. I will live for You and do Your will. Thank you for saving my soul and making a place in Heaven for me.

Chapter 8

THE FALLEN

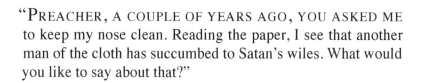

"PREACHER, A COUPLE OF YEARS AGO, YOU ASKED ME to keep my nose clean. Reading the paper, I see that another man of the cloth has succumbed to Satan's wiles. What would you like to say about that?"

Preacher turned around in his seat. "Hebrews 8:12 says 'For I will forgive their wickedness and will remember their sins no more.' You tell me, does that specify forgiveness only comes before you are saved?"

"Christians love to see souls saved. However, if that same individual later allows Satan to use them, most Christians wag their tongue and write them off. Moses saw miracles like the burning bush and still fell to pride. He asked forgiveness, and God allowed him to keep leading His people. Peter learned at the feet of Jesus yet denied Him three times and cursed. After forgiveness, God used this cursing fisherman to change the world.

"It should not shock us when leaders fail. This has happened since the beginning of time. It can happen to anyone who lets his guard down and considers temptations as human matters instead of spiritual warfare. The question remains—did you ask for forgiveness?

Matthew 7:1-2: *Judge not, that ye be not judged. For with what judgement ye judge, ye shall be judge'*

I thought of the story of the little boy visiting his grandparents on their farm. They gave him a slingshot to play with in the woods. The boy practiced but could never hit the target. Getting a little discouraged, he headed back for dinner. As he was walking back, he saw Grandma's pet duck. Just out of impulse, he let the slingshot fly, hitting the duck square in the head and killing it. He was shocked and grieved. In a panic, he hid the dead duck in the woodpile, only to see his sister watching. Sally had seen it all, but she said nothing.

After lunch, the next day, Grandma said, "Sally, let's wash the dishes." But Sally said, "Grandma, Johnny told me he wanted to help in the kitchen." Then she whispered to him, "Remember the duck?" So, Johnny did the dishes. Later that day, Grandpa asked the children if they wanted to go fishing and Grandma said, "I'm sorry, but I need Sally to help make supper." Sally just smiled and said, "Well, that's all right because Johnny told me he wanted to help." She whispered again, "Remember the duck?" So, Sally went fishing and Johnny stayed to help.

After several days of Johnny doing both his chores and Sally's, he finally could not stand it any longer. He came to Grandma and confessed that he had killed the duck. Grandma knelt down, gave him a hug, and said, "Sweetheart, I know. I was standing at the window and saw the whole thing, but because I love you, I forgave you. I was just wondering how long you would let Sally make a slave of you."

Whatever is in your past, whatever you have done, the devil keeps throwing it up in your face (lying, cheating, debt, fear, bad habits, hatred, anger, bitterness, etc.). Whatever your sins, you need to know that God was standing at the window and saw everything. He has seen your whole life and wants you to know that He loves you and that you are forgiven. He is wondering how long you will let the devil make a slave of you.

The wonderful thing about God is when you ask for forgiveness, He not only forgives you but also forgets. It is by God's grace and mercy that we are saved.

When the prodigal son returned, his father put on his finger a ring, covered him with a robe, placed new shoes on his feet, and killed the fatted calf. He did not ask him where he had been. He did not ask him what he had done. He was overjoyed that his son came back. *"For this my son was dead, and is alive again; he was lost and is found"* (Luke 1 5:24).

Perhaps you are like the prodigal son. God says, come home, just as you are.

Chapter 9

THE PAST

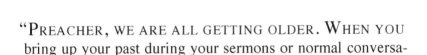

"PREACHER, WE ARE ALL GETTING OLDER. WHEN YOU bring up your past during your sermons or normal conversations, do many say you're living in the past?"

"Well," Preacher said, "you want to know something? The Israelites laid up stones for remembrance of important happenings. God gave us a clear biblical warrant for recounting the great events of the past. It is a very biblical thing to do. It is the right thing to do. We ought to do it for the benefit of our own generation. We ought to do it so we can hear those stories. Trying to do away with the past is the first thing communists do to take over a country.

"Some have been in this church for years and years and have never heard the stories from the past. They have not been told of the struggles, the buildings, and the fabulous blessings that God has bestowed on the Akron Baptist Temple. We also ought to do it for the benefit of the generations yet to come. God knew the danger of forgetting the past and told them to wear His word on their sleeves and to tell children of His miracles.

"We can accept it or not. The way we view our past and remember it will affect our future. It shows we can learn from the past. It shows us from where He has brought us and where we might have been. I believe it is Satan's business to destroy history."

The Romans had a mythical god called Janus, the god of beginnings and endings. He is usually depicted as having two faces pointing in opposite direction since he looks to the future and to the past. We look spiritually to what we owe the past and what we owe the future. We owe the past an appreciation of those who accomplished so much before us.

We have heard many stories of the beginning of this church. In fact, many of you recall the past and lived through this segment of time. In June 1934, a small group of men and women joined Dallas F. Billington, at Rimer school, on Manchester road, Akron. Ohio and together they felt an urging in their hearts and a moving of God's Spirit to establish a church in Akron, Ohio. It would be free of denominational control and would focus on preaching the word of God and the gospel of Jesus Christ, as well as a strong commitment to world missions.

We owe to the past fidelity to the heritage we have been given. We are morally obligated to respect that great body of Christian teaching which has been given to us and to refuse to compromise it. We owe to the future to repeat the mighty works of God, for the benefit of generations yet to come.

The danger of forgetting the past was born out in the Old Testament after the death of Joshua. By a series of great military victories, he led the people of God into the promised land. As long as he was alive, the nation served the Lord, but things changed after he died. We pick up the story in Judges 2:6. The people served God as long as the elders who were with Joshua were alive, because those elders could recount the great works of God. And God said to write them in a book for remembrance. However, after that entire generation had been gathered to their fathers, another generation grew up who knew neither the Lord nor what he had done for Israel. Then the Israelites did evil in the eyes of the Lord and served baalim (false gods).

We are living in a day in which the younger generation has no sense of history. Today we see them tearing down statues with no consciousness of the history and heritage of our nation, or the God-fearing people that suffered and died for the land of the free and the home of the brave. They fail to realize the blessings of God on this nation and that He allowed this heritage to be passed down to us.

Sometimes, we look at history and think we are the first ones on the face of the earth ever to do anything good. There is no sense of what came before us. Examples from the Old Testament show what happens when the people of God forget their heritage. They end up in bondage, slavery, decline, and idolatry.

We saw the decline of the Akron Baptist Temple. Like the story of Joshua, we saw its history and heritage dissolved by another generation who knew not the biblical testimony, nor what God had done for its people. We ought to recount the great works of God to our children and to our children's children and on to the third, fourth and fifth generations. We ought to keep telling these stories over and over, just as God commanded Israel.

Now we have the New Testament. Does that mean we should discard the Old Testament? Heaven forbid. Jesus said, "I come not to destroy but to fulfill" (Matt. 5:17). We owe it to the future to keep the best of the past while changing to meet the needs of the future. John Kennedy said, "Change amid conflict is not progress."

This church has changed a lot over the past years. It would amaze the people who founded this church to see what we are now. I do not know what our founders would think if they came into our service today. What would happen if they somehow stumbled into our sanctuary while the band was playing? When they heard that rock style music, they might think they are on another planet.

A few years ago, the Pro Football Hall of Fame game was on TV. Before the game, they inducted that year's inductees into the Hall of Fame. While most read from a preprinted paper, Terry Bradshaw, quarterback of the Pittsburgh Steelers during their Super Bowl years, gave an emotional talk. Without notes, it was Terry Bradshaw, the country boy from Louisiana, talking.

He said, "This is a great moment for me. A lot of people thought I would never make it in the NFL. I barely got into college. I flunked my ACT. I barely got in. When I graduated from college, pro scouts said, 'This kid's never going to play pro ball.' But the Steelers took a chance on me. The first year we went 1-14. It looked like I did not have any career at all.

"Then they drafted Lynn Swann and John Stallworth and Franco Harris and Rocky Bleier, and all those guys. We had Mike Webster up front, and that steel curtain defense, and all the pieces fell in place, and we began to win. It was all of them that made me, and why I am here today."

Then Terry Bradshaw told the story of how he liked to play. "You know, I was so close to my players and fans. There was an emotional bond between us. You are nothing and nothing in this world matters if people don't love you and if you don't love people. If you have love in your life, the rest of it does not really matter."

On the very first play after an interception, Bradshaw would call the signals, drop back ten yards and send Lynn Swann down the one side and John Stallworth down the other side. No short passes here. He would throw the ball about sixty yards down the field. Every time the Steelers got the ball, they would throw a long ball down the field.

At his Hall of Fame induction, Terry Bradshaw said, "I played aggressively. Why play any other way? We were always throwing the ball long. Anybody can throw it short."

Our church forefathers taught us a lesson—to throw long. What a lesson that is for us as we contemplate the future. We owe it to the future to throw the ball long, way down the field for Jesus Christ. We owe it to the future to throw the ball long because that is what the people who came before us did. That means no small plans. No small dreams. No small ideas. I only want to hear about big things and big dreams and big ideas and big goals.

Dallas told Stanley Bond, the Sunday school superintendent, "We are going to build the largest Sunday school." He told the choir director, "You fill the choir, and I will fill the church."

We owe it to the future to throw the ball long. Anybody can throw it short. We owe it to the past, present, and future to be bold and aggressive as we reach out with God's help to take our entire region for Jesus Christ. We all know there are just as many people in Akron today that need Jesus as there ever was—maybe more.

So, I say it again—throw the long ball, anybody can throw it short.

Psalm 145:4 says, "*One generation shall commend your works to another. They will tell of your mighty acts.*" How many generations have there been in the church so far? Each generation contributes a chapter, and the chapters together make up a book of God's praise, a book of the mighty works of God. We are busy writing our chapter in the book of God's praise; we must take what we have been given and pass it on to the next generation.

The Christian life is not a marathon; it is a relay race. Paul said, *"I have fought a good fight, I have finished my course, I have kept the faith."* (2 Timothy 4:7) Others before us ran their race and handed the baton to us; we are commanded to run as fast as we can, then hand it off to the next generation.

Heavenly Father, we thank you for what you have done. We are awestruck at the stories we hear of how you have worked in the past. You are the same God. We have the same Bible, the same Jesus, the same gospel. Do in our day what you did in the days of our fathers, that we might see your mighty hand at work. Help us be bold that we might reach out with the gospel to this entire region and, in turn, reach the world. Then we shall turn the baton over to the next generation. Amen.

The Lord bless thee, and keep thee,

> *The Lord make his face to shine upon thee, and begracious unto thee, The Lord lift up his countenance upon thee and give thee peace.*
> (Numbers 6:24-26)

May God richly bless you and give you a great day in the Lord.

Chapter 10

WHOSE FAULT

"Preacher, did you see that blurb the other day In the Akron Beacon Journal where the guy was speeding, had an accident, and blamed God for his wife's death?"

"Well," Preacher said, "it's not the first time someone became angry with God, whether a Christian or not, and it will not be the last time for one to feel the urge to blame God. Many times, in our pain, we are prone to point a finger and raise a fist at Heaven. Martha said to Jesus, *'If you had been here, my brother would not have died'* (John 11:21KJV). Our question should not be, Why God? but, what are you trying to tell me? God is never the one to blame for our pain, but the one we turn to for help."

> *"Come to me, all who are weary and heavy-laden, and I will give you rest"* (Matt. 11:28 KJV).

"It's not my fault." Have you ever heard anyone say that? I remember the comic strip Family Circus. Whenever something bad happened, one of the kids would say, "It's not my fault!" In one strip, there was a shadowy figure with the name 'Not My

Fault' written on the back of his shirt, and he was complaining, "I get blamed for everything around here!"

Whether the issue is physical, financial, or spiritual, the response of some people will always be, "It's not my fault." We live during a time when people are unwilling to take personal responsibility for their own lives, for their own welfare, health, or spiritual growth. If they are unhealthy, it is because no one made them exercise. (I have always said if God wanted me to touch my toes, He would have put them on my knees.) If they lack a marketable skill, it is because no one guided them in their career choices. If they are immature Christians, it's because the church didn't have the right discipleship programs, or the preacher didn't preach the right sermons, or because, "Momma didn't pray with me before I went to bed every night. It's not my fault!"

When they fail to take personal responsibility for their own life and the results of their choices begin to crystallize, there is a tendency to look for someone else to blame. However, when we stand before God and the judgment seat of Christ, we will answer for our own failures and the choices we made. Robert Greenleaf wrote that 'Every man is a monument to the choices he has made.'

Recently, the pastor of a mega-church gave in to the lust of the flesh and embraced a different lifestyle. He admitted it and expected his congregation to accept him because it's not his fault. In his words, God made him that way. He accepted no responsibility for choices he has made, or the lusts he has given himself over to, or the downward spiral of his moral and spiritual state. He points to Heaven and says, "This is God's choice for my life. If it is anyone's fault, it's His fault."

2 Peter 1:10 says, *"Therefore, brethren, be even more diligent to make your call and election sure, for if you do these things you will never fall, and you will receive a rich welcome into the eternal kingdom of our Lord and Savior Jesus Christ."* This verse rejects the worldview that claims, "It's not my fault," and exhorts us to take personal responsibility for our own spiritual growth and maturity as a believer. He issues this imperative, *"Grow in grace and in the knowledge of our Lord and Savior Jesus Christ"* (2 Pet. 3:18 KJV).

Over the years, and more so recently, we have watched great men and women of faith, fail and fall to sin. When they have fallen and face humiliation, they inevitably say, "It's not my fault. If only someone had called me or helped me. It is my parent's fault. It is the church's fault. It is the pastor's fault. It is the media's fault. It is somebody's fault, but it is not my fault!"

Not getting on the scales does not mean we have not gained weight. When we refuse to investigate the mirror of God's Word, we have already lost ground. We must take personal responsibility for our own spiritual maturity and must never fall into the trap of saying, "It's not my fault." Those words will carry no weight when we stand before the judgment seat of Christ.

A small boy stood on the family cat's tail. The mother, hearing the terrible outburst from the cat, called from the next room, "Tommy, stop pulling that cat's tail!" Tommy yelled back, "I'm not pulling the cat's tail. I am standing on it. The cat is doing the pulling!" That kid would make a good politician.

Is this not what Adam and Eve did in the Garden of Eden in Genesis 3:12-13? Adam blamed God for his sin because God gave him that woman, Eve, then he blamed Eve for giving him the fruit. Eve blamed the serpent for their wrongdoing and the serpent didn't have a leg to stand on.

An elderly man, recently widowed and retired, wanted to buy a motor home and see America. He had not bought a car in over twenty years. A sales rep was showing him the various features of an RV, and as he was explaining all the features, the man asked, "What does this button do?" The sales rep said, "That's the cruise control. Get this big boy rolling down the highway, press that button, and it drives by itself."

They decided to take a test drive. The two of them took off down the highway with the sales rep behind the wheel, explaining all the wonderful RV features. The rep said, "Sir, would you like to drive for a while?" The elderly man said, "That would be nice." They stopped, switched places, and drove off. All was going well, and the sales rep told the man he was going to the back of the RV to stretch out on the couch and enjoy the ride.

He had just closed his eyes for a catnap when he heard a voice say, "What kind of mileage does this thing get?" The sales rep looked up in horror to see the old man sitting on a chair beside him. He spluttered out, "Who's driving?" The old man said, "Oh, don't worry, I've got it on cruise control." The sales rep dashed for the driver's seat, but he was too late. The RV came to a sharp curve in the road, went straight through it, down an embankment, across a cornfield, and wrapped itself around an enormous oak tree.

Well, the sales rep had the RV towed back to the salesroom. When they got there, the owner of the dealership looked in horror to see this beautiful RV totally smashed. He said, "What in the world happened?" The old man said, "The cruise control doesn't work."

That gentleman exhibited a problem we have in society today that I call the "It's-not-my-fault syndrome." We have excuses for everything. An obscene phone caller has an "uncontrollable impulse disorder." A man walks into the office of the Mayor of San Francisco, shoots him dead, and then gives a "Twinkie defense", saying sugar made him do it. Who is to blame?

We sometimes use the blame game when we look at the younger generation and say, "What is this world coming to?" (Do not tell me you have not said that.) There are times I think we all have been guilty of trying to put the fault on others.

We read in the paper and hear on the air,
      Of killing and stealing and crime everywhere.
We sigh and say, as we notice the trend,
"This young generation... Where will it end?"
But can we be sure it is their fault alone?
Are we less guilty, who places in their way?
Too many things that lead them astray.
Too much money, too much idle time.
Too many movies of passion and crime.
Too many books not fit to be read.
Too much evil in what they hear said.
Too many children encouraged to roam.
Too many parents who will not stay home.
(LISTEN)
    Kids don't make the movies; they don't write the books.
     They don't paint the pictures of gangsters and crooks.
      They don't make the liquor; they don't run the bars.
    They don't make the laws, and they don't make the cars.
      They don't peddle the drugs that muddle the brain.
That is all done by older folks, greedy for gain.
Delinquent teenagers: oh, how we condemn
The sins of the nation and blame it on them.
      By the laws of the blameless, the Savior made known.

Who is among us to cast the first stone?
For in so many cases, it is sad, but it is true,
Maybe it's not their fault, perhaps it's me and you
(Taken from an article by Ron Hutchcraft))

It was not your fault you lost your job; it was not your fault for the sickness; it was not your fault for the death of your loved one, the divorce, or when your spouse walked away. Exodus 22:23 says, *"If you afflict them in any way, and they cry at all unto me, I will surely hear their cry."*

Friend, God is waiting to hear your cry for help. It was not Joseph's fault he was thrown into the pit or sold into slavery, but God heard his cry, knew his faithfulness, and promoted him from the pit to the palace. Likewise, God knows it was not your fault. God is still on the throne. He wants to hear from you, so He can bless and promote you.

It may have been your fault, someone else's fault, or a bit of both. Either way, God says, "Call upon me in the day of trouble: I will deliver thee, and thou shalt glorify me." (Psalm 50:15) He wants to bless you. Just ask forgiveness and be faithful.

We must stop blaming God for the messes we put ourselves in, since it was we that made poor choices and awful decisions. It was we that chose to go left when God said to go right. Instead of blaming God, we all need to ask Him for forgiveness and for the direction to improve our lives.

> *"For I know the plans I have for you, declares the Lord, plans to prosper you and not to harm you, plans to give you hope and a future"* (Jer. 29:11 KJV).

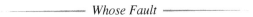

Our heavenly Father, you have said, "I want to bless you, not hurt you." God, you have said if we ask for forgiveness and are faithful, you will bless us without regard to fault.

Chapter 11

LIFE'S MISFORTUNES

"PREACHER, I'M SURE YOU HAVE TALKED TO MANY people you know to be Christians who experience serious misfortunes in their life. They may even ask God why He would permit such things happening to a Christian, or why He is punishing them. What do you tell them?"

"First," Preacher said, "if they have been born again, God cannot punish them. He has already put all the punishment on His Son, the Lord Jesus Christ. Jesus paid their sin debt on the cross for yesterday, today, and tomorrow. As a child of God, He only wants good for you.

"Secondly, I tell them of the blind man, blind from birth. The disciples asked Jesus who sinned—him or his parents—to cause his blindness. Jesus answered, '*Neither this man sinned nor his parents. On the contrary, he was born blind that the works of God might be revealed in him*' (John 9:1-3). This is confirmed in Romans 8:28, '*And we know that all things work together for good to them that love God, to them who are the called according to His purpose.*' It does not say everything that happens to us is good; it says, 'all things work together for good."

My question: If you stub your toe on a chair and in your anguished and pain, your wife laughs at you (tell the truth) what would your words of wisdom be? "Oh, Thank you, Lord." (Oh Yeah)

This may be an extremely poor illustration for the misfortunes and calamities that people endure, because we have trouble seeing how these happenings are good.

> 1Thessalonians 5:16-18, *"Rejoice evermore. Pray without ceasing. In everything give thanks: for this is the will of God in Christ Jesus concerning you."*

We learned from Jesus to give thanks first. His miracles were performed after He said thanks. Remember before He told Lazarus to come forth from the grave, the Bible says, (John 11:41) *"Then they took away the stone from the place where the dead was laid and Jesus lifted up his eyes and said, Father, I thank thee that thou hast heard me."*

Perhaps Jesus is teaching us when misfortunes happen, we are to first give thanks to God for His will to be done and He will hear us.

A painting of a burned-out log cabin in the middle of the woods hung in an art gallery. All that remained of the cabin was the chimney, a few logs with red embers, and wisps of smoke. In the front of the cabin, stood an old man with one thumb hung on his bib overalls. His other handheld the hand of a small child in pajamas. The boy clutched a teddy bear in the crook of his arm as he wiped away tears. In the middle of this misfortune, presumably with everything gone, the caption read, 'Hush child. Don't weep. God ain't dead.'

This picture reminds us that in our deepest sorrows, all is not lost; God is alive and well. Yes, the Good News: In faith, we can move through the trials of life with confidence and hope.

Several books and articles have been written about, "Why do bad things happen to good people?" I believe they have all missed the point. Why do bad things happen to good people? Because they are not good. How do I know that? Like the children's song says, "The Bible tells me so."

> *"As it is written, there is none righteous, no, not one"* (Rom. 3:10). *"But we are all as an unclean thing, and all our righteousness's are as filthy rags"* (Isa. 64:6).

We also find in Matthew 5:45, *"And sendeth rain on the just and on the unjust."* If, after we were saved, nothing bad happened to us, then certain people would want to be saved just for this reason. Then they would not be asking by faith, and you can only be saved by faith.

This topic of bad things happening to good people is brought up often. Perhaps it can be better illustrated by looking at a biblical event. Open your Bible and read Mark 4:35-41. Jesus had been teaching all day, and the disciples must have been on an evangelistic high. Jesus told them to get in the boat and pass to the other side. They got in the boat after the sermon, doing exactly as the Lord said. Not only were they in the will of God, but Jesus is in the boat with them going to the other side. However, while in the will of God and in the presence of Jesus, there is a problem. A fierce, sudden wind kicks up and waves of water crash into the boat. Despite obeying God's will and doing His command, they run into the largest storm of their lives.

Likewise, you can be in the will of God, following His command and still find yourself in the largest storm of your life. You may feel like you are going under at any minute. Note that there were other boats in the same storm, but Jesus was not in those other boats. The storm treated everyone the same way. Philosophically, you will experience storms where you cannot control the wind or the waves even though you are in His will.

The Bible says the disciples were scared. When we experience difficult circumstances such as financial hardship, sickness, or death, our emotions run scared. Like the disciples, we say, "God, where are you? God, don't you care?" Or like Martha and Mary said, "Lord, *if thou hadst been here, my brother had not died*." (John 11:32) We question God. Jesus said, "Let's go to the other side." *Then He said,* "Why are you so fearful? How is it you have no faith?" *(*Mark 4:40 KJV).

Just like the disciples, we have the tendency to focus on the problem instead of focusing on the promise. We need to be saturated with God's promises and let Jesus handle the problems. He has said, *"Lo I am with you always even unto the end of the world"* (Matt. 28:20).

God is always with us; He is in the same boat. He lives in our hearts and the Holy Spirit will awaken (or hear us) when we call upon Him. The storm can increase your faith and give purpose to a close relationship with God. Remember, when you are down to nothing, He is up to something. The only way God can show He is in control, is by putting us into situations we cannot control.

Part 2
CONFERENCES

.

Chapter 12

ABOUT OTHERS

THE MODERATOR SAID, "FIRST, EACH OF YOU HERE
has built a church because you have felt it was God's will and
felt you could not accomplish it without God's help. Would you
elaborate, in a few words, what else you feel to be instrumental
in your church's physical and spiritual growth?"

Preacher, Charles, and I were attending a pastoral conference
in Columbus, Ohio. This was the question asked by the moderator to three of the pastors on the platform at the beginning of
the morning session. The first one gave thanks to his wife and
other close relatives for their support. There was light applause
when he sat down.

The second pastor explained how he had previously worked for
a construction company and that workers plus materials were
supplied at cost. Then he told how he had worked day and night
to develop the church like he wanted. The moderator had asked
if they could tell their story in a few words. I felt I would have
introduced the second speaker by saying, "And now gentlemen,
the next man needs no introduction, just an ending." They gave
him light applause as well.

Preacher rose from his seat and approached the podium with his Bible in hand. He raised the Bible in the air, leaned into the microphone and said one word, "Others" Then he returned to his seat.

It was silent; there was no applause. I was sitting in the front row and turned around to see every head bowed and some hands raised. The Holy Spirit had taken one word to touch the hearts of the other pastors and instill in them a sermon they would never forget. It was a word that could only be understood by a born-again believer who was 'all-in' for the Lord. *"That is, that I may be comforted together with you by the mutual faith both of you and me"* (Rom. 1:12 KJV).

We can expound on, "others."

C. S. Lewis said, "Humility is not thinking less of yourself; it's thinking of yourself less."

Jesus said, "If I be lifted up from the earth, will draw all men unto me." (John12:32)

Danny Thomas said, "Success has nothing to do with what you gain in life or accomplish. It is what you do for others.

Calvin Coolidge stated, "No person was ever honored for what they received but what they gave."

God gave His Son. His Son gave His life. All we can do is give ourselves.

Poet John Donne wrote, "No man is an island," arguing for the interconnectedness of all people with God.

Preacher understood this when he instructed his Sunday school superintendent, Stanly Bond, to build up the Sunday school because the kids would have to have their parents bring them there. He also told his choir director you fill the choir, and I can fill the church.

Chapter 13

HEAVEN

"WHAT ARE YOUR VIEWS ON HEAVEN?"

It was lunchtime at the Bible conference. Heaven had been the topic of the last speaker before lunch. We sat at a table for eight, which included some of the most well-known attendees, and were having a round robin discussion on Heaven. One person could not wait to see his wife again. To the minister in a wheelchair, Heaven meant running down the streets of gold.

One pastor told the old story of the speaker preaching on Heaven. Halfway through the sermon, he was getting more exuberant, and exclaimed, "Every one that wants to go to Heaven, on your feet." One lone man stayed seated. "Don't you want to go to Heaven?" the preacher asked. "Well, yeah," the man said, "but I thought you were getting up a load tonight."

When the chuckling died down, Preacher said, "Well gentleman, I say anyone that does not want to see Jesus first, may need to go back down to the altar. Jesus is the only reason we make it to Heaven. He suffered and died on the cross for our

sins. I don't know about you, but I can't wait to thank him."
Everyone said, "Amen!"

*"For now, we see through a glass darkly; but
then face to face"* (1Cor. 13:12 KJV).

Some ministers and other born-again believers think of all the
advantages of our Heavenly home and lose sight of the fact
that Jesus is there, and He is the only reason we are going there.

Some believe that is why we are saved, just to go to Heaven.
However, the last command Jesus gave his disciples was this;
*"Therefore go and make disciples of all nations, baptizing them
in the name of the Father and of the Son and of the Holy Spirit,
and teaching them to obey everything I have commanded you."*
(Matthew 28:19-20) We are saved to serve.

Some make the gospel only about Heaven and Hell. Perhaps it
would be better to preach the gospel about life and death.

The fear of Hell will not save you; it is knowing Jesus as your
personal savior that will save you.

I feel the same as preacher. I recall the words in the song, "I
Bowed on my Knees and Cried Holy." The second verse says:

As I entered the gates of that city,
My loved ones all knew me well
They took me down the streets of Heaven;
Such scenes where too many to tell,
I saw Abraham, Jacob and Isaac,
Talked with Mark, and Timothy
But I said, "I want to see Jesus,
Cause he's the one who died for me."

Chapter 14

ONE BOOK

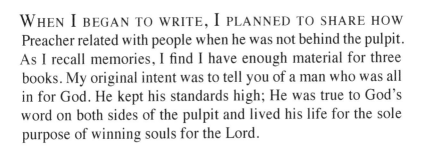

WHEN I BEGAN TO WRITE, I PLANNED TO SHARE HOW
Preacher related with people when he was not behind the pulpit.
As I recall memories, I find I have enough material for three
books. My original intent was to tell you of a man who was all
in for God. He kept his standards high; He was true to God's
word on both sides of the pulpit and lived his life for the sole
purpose of winning souls for the Lord.

I then realized the number of stories to be told of actual con-
versions away from the church. The many lives that preacher
directed to Christ by not being ashamed of the gospel.

Then thirdly with my constant questions I obtained a Christian
education better than a Bible seminary could offer. I gained
knowledge that assisted me in living a Christian life in the real
world and have many stories relative to assisting in the building
of two other churches.

Preacher said many times that God did not send him to Akron
to build tires, but to build a church. I discovered God sent
me to Alabama to build a church in a city that had fourteen

Southern Baptist churches. There was a need for an Independent Baptist church. I understand they have just finished their third expansion.

A few years later, my company sent me to Brussels, Belgium to build two plants for plastic processing. I soon came to realize that it was God who sent me, for there were 25,000 English-speaking people in Brussels who had no church home to go too on Sunday mornings. The other churches conducted services in French or Flemish. I encountered many experiences involved in establishing an English-speaking church. I taught the adult bible class until we hired two full time ministers.

I do not believe you can write a Christian book without telling the reader if they have never asked for forgiveness of their sin, they need Jesus. So, it turns out to be three books in one. This book shows how one man, dedicated to God, can hold on to his Christian standards, encourage others to keep their faith, and listen to the still small voice of God, while advising others how to keep their soul out of hell.

Chapter 15

PREACHING AND POLITICS

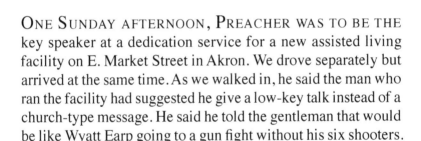

ONE SUNDAY AFTERNOON, PREACHER WAS TO BE THE key speaker at a dedication service for a new assisted living facility on E. Market Street in Akron. We drove separately but arrived at the same time. As we walked in, he said the man who ran the facility had suggested he give a low-key talk instead of a church-type message. He said he told the gentleman that would be like Wyatt Earp going to a gun fight without his six shooters.

In attendance were the Mayor, several councilmen, and other dignitaries. They each gave their political speeches. The one councilman said his mother was living in the facility, and he visited as often as he could. I sang, "If We Never Meet Again." Preacher rose and started by saying, "There will come a time when we will visit our loved ones for the last time. If we never see them again here on this earth, will we ever see them again? We can if we have made our peace with God."

He then told the gathering that when he was growing up, he desired to be governor of Kentucky. He obtained every book he could get his hands on about government operations and how others worked to get elected. Then he told how something happened and he met Jesus. After that, his desires and energy in life was to preach Christ and to tell the world we were born into sin.

> '*And the wages of sin is death, but the gift of God is eternal life through Jesus Christ our Lord*' (Rom. 6:23 KJV).

Preacher said," We are in some ways alike. This morning your efforts are in getting elected and then building a kingdom based on your ideas and desires. Let's just call it the Kingdom of Akron. I take what I have learned about building a government and adding that to the calling I received from God and use everything in my being to build the Kingdom of God. Even our methods in recruiting are similar. The Bible says in Matthew 6:33,'*But seek you first the kingdom of God and his righteousness and all these things shall be added unto you,* and John 3:3 says, *verily, verily, I say unto thee, except a man be born again , he cannot see the kingdom of God.*"

I have found that politicians and preachers are a lot alike. They believe in what they do, persevere no matter the situation, and cannot wait to tell others of their decision. They feel so enthused they invite others to join them. Also, there are many who resent them, who do not want to discuss politics or religion. They can serve their constituents or God for forty years without appreciation but let them make one poor decision and people want to hang them. A person cannot serve long before realizing this.

Have you noticed every political question is becoming a social question, and every social question is becoming a religious question?

After his message, they met Preacher with great enthusiasm and fellowship. By drawing his analogy, he made them feel like they were all on the same page. He not only told the congregation about Jesus and how to be saved but opened a long-lasting friendship with the mayor and councilmen.

Chapter 16

ALMOST HOME

IT WAS SATURDAY EVENING. I HAD BEEN ASKED TO
sing at the Sunday school teachers' banquet. Before performing,
I told them I usually only sing, but to use one of Preacher's say-
ings, "Let me tell you something—this is a true story. I read it
in the paper."

It was July 1952 on Catalina Island, off the coast of California.
Florence Chadwick waded into the freezing water to swim the
channel to the coast. It was going to be tough. She could barely
see the escort boat that accompanied her in the dense fog, and
there were sharks. She swam for fifteen hours before asking
them to be pull her from the water.

Ms. Chadwick had done this kind of thing before. She was a
long-distance swimmer and had been the first woman to swim
the English Channel in both directions. On this day, though, all
she could see was fog. Exhausted and discouraged, she thought,
I cannot do this, I cannot make it. Florence gave up. She learned
later she was less than a mile from her goal. A few days later,
the media interviewed her. She said, "I'm not excusing myself,
but if I had only been able to see the land, I might have made it."

What was it that caused Florence to give up that day? Was it the cold water, exhaustion, or fear? No, the reason she failed to reach her goal was the fog. Two months later, she swam that same Catalina channel and set a new speed record. Once again, the water was cold and the fog was heavy, but she said she created a mental picture of the land just in sight and held it in her mind.

Sometimes in our lives we meet up with a fog called despair, that awful feeling that we are stuck, unable to move ahead because of some event or hurt we are struggling with. This is a vital subject. The dictionary says despair is "a state in which all hope is lost, or absent—the feeling that everything is wrong, and nothing will turn out well." Despair means to "abandon hope, give up, lose heart—and feel disappointed, frustrated, rejected or condemned."

When you feel despair, put in your mind a mental picture of Jesus standing on the shore of Heaven with outstretched arms saying, *"Come unto me all ye that labor and are heavy laden, and I will give you rest"* (Matt. 11:28 KJV).

Otherwise, you could say the words of this song:

"Almost Home but Lost"
People passing on their way
To the end of this short life
Never looking up to Jesus
To relieve their sinful strife
Never caring that their life
May be almost gone
Never knowing that they're so close
Yes, Almost Home, But Lost

After the banquet, Preacher requested that the choir director put that song on the program Sunday morning directly before the message. On Sunday morning, I sang the song. Preacher walked to the pulpit and said, "Let me tell you something. This is a true story. Not long ago you may have read it in the Akron Beacon Journal." He told the story of Florence Chadwick.

At the end of the service he said, "You don't know when your time is through. No matter how close to heaven you think you are, if you have not asked forgiveness for your sins when your time comes, you will be lost. Lost in eternity forever, because with God you will not get a second chance to face the fog like Florence Chadwick did. *"And as it is appointed unto men once to die, but after this the Judgement"* (Heb. 9:27 KJV).

Most of the time, Preacher and I did not discuss the song I would sing before his message. He felt the Holy Spirit would lead. Several times though, while in route to a service, he would ask me what I plan on singing and I would find later that his whole sermon was built around that song.

When I quit singing hillbilly songs and started singing gospel, I prayed to be used of God in whatever way possible. Just as preacher had told me, I found I could not stand before an audience on my own. By listening to the still small voice of God, I received my blessing by knowing I was on the same wave link as the preacher and God. What anyone else thought of my singing did not matter.
There were times, as with the Florence Chadwick story and other song picks, I could not help thinking that maybe preacher was praying for a sermon topic and God sent the answer through me.

This became evident when on occasions I sang a song I had written. Because God gave me a new song, no one including

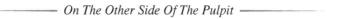

preacher had ever heard it before. He would sometimes say afterwards, "I was wondering how I should end the message and the words of your song came through loud and clear. Preacher's most requested song was "The King is Coming."

Part 3

ONE ON ONE

Chapter 17

THE WAITRESS

"You look like you might be having a bad hair day, "Preacher said.

We were traveling to a sister church for a Sunday evening meeting and decided to stop for sandwiches so we would not get the grumbellies during the service. Our waitress looked flustered and troubled. She took our order without a smile or any small talk. When she brought our food, she still appeared disheveled. We received part of our order and prayed while the waitress went to get the rest. She finished setting down the food and ask if there was anything else.

We began to eat and Preacher said, "Little lady, you look like you might be having a bad hair day."

The waitress said, "I cannot believe everything that's happened to me today. I could write a book about it. I wish there were someone who could help me."

Preacher said, "Little lady, you can tell me all the things you have been through if you want, but I can't help you." There was an extended pause. "But I know someone who can." Then he told her about Jesus. He said, "Now listen, all you have to do is go back in the kitchen and find a quiet spot and say, 'Jesus, please forgive me of all my sins. I want you to take over my life.' If you say that in faith believing, you will be born again, and then you can ask Him to help you."

We finished our meal and preacher picked up the guest check and went to the checkout desk. There was no one attending the cash register and we waited for what we considered a long period of time. When the man came to the desk, he took the check from preachers' hand and impaled it on the paid spindle. He said, "Thanks preacher. I just went into the kitchen and my daughter was crying. I asked her if the men she was serving hurt her feelings. She said, 'no, the one guy said he was a Baptist preacher and God could help me. So, I asked for forgiveness and I just feel good all over.' I have been praying for her for years.

Preacher, whenever you are by this way you can stop in for a free meal anytime."

Chapter 18
THE ATTENDANT

"DO YOU LIVE AROUND HERE?" PREACHER ASKED THE gas station attendant.

We were headed to Cincinnati, Ohio. Between Columbus and Cincinnati on Route 71, we stopped in a small town for gas. The attendant came out to the car from the garage and Charles Billington, Dallas's son, told him to fill-it-up. I do not expect the younger reader to grasp this, as gas stations are self-service now. The attendant took off the gas cap and placed the hose in the gas pipe. He then opened the hood, checked the oil, checked the water, kicked the tires, and washed the windows. Believe it or not, this is the way it used to be done. However, each generation feels they can do things better. So, we do these tasks ourselves. It is called progress.

We all got out to stretch our legs. Preacher asked the attendant, "Do you live around here?"

The attendant said, "Oh yeah, I was born here and have lived here all my life. It's a great place and I ain't ever going anyplace else."

Preacher said, "Well, son, I hate to break your bubble, but the truth is, someday you're going to leave this place permanently. Which direction you go, you and you alone will have to decide."

Charles, Clyde White, and I headed into the garage to get a soft drink while preacher spoke with the attendant.

We got our soft drinks and headed back to the car. That Black man was kneeling between the pumps and gave his heart to Christ.

I am sorry, but my righteous indignation rose above sea level when I read the news article a short time ago about the sale of the church, which stated the Akron Baptist Temple was founded on segregation. In another paragraph it reads, "The Akron Baptist Temple was led by the late Rev. Dallas F. Billington, known, in part, for his strong support of segregation."

It would appear the reporter who wrote this segment only knew of this information by viewing a video produced by Pastor Ed Holland which talks about the first Rev. Billington's prejudice, saying he was a product of his Kentucky roots, which "slanted him to segregation." It further states, "It's something our church has repented of." The church had nothing to repent of.

The aforementioned statements are nothing more than a heterogenous conglomeration of absurdity, intended to bamboozle the anatomy of individuals into intoxication by their abominable and irresistible powers of suggestibility. Nothing could be further from the truth.

A person only needed to be around preacher a short period of time to realize it did not matter about another person's size, position, wealth, sex, education or the color of his skin. His concern was about that person's soul and where would they spend eternity.

This was obvious when it concerned the black gas station attendant. How many other people that day and days before had stopped at that location and their only concern was to get gas and how quickly could it be pumped. As preacher often said, Jesus cares and I do too.

You could always see this concern on preacher's face and feel it in his words when he spoke to groups. Often, they were predominantly black.

Perhaps the one who needs to repent is Rev. Holland.

If you fill your mind with God's word, there will be no room for Satan's lies.

Chapter 19

LADY OF THE NIGHT

"CAN I HELP YOU?"

We had finished an evening service in a small church southwest of Akron. Most of the roads were only two lanes. Preacher was extremely tired, so we changed places so he could stretch out in the back seat and rest. To make matters worse, the road was closed, and we had to take an alternate route. What was already going to be a long way home was now going to be longer.

Most everything had closed. We finally found a truck stop and decided to get a midnight snack. We pulled in and parked between the building and the eighteen wheelers.

Preacher stayed in the car and we went in and picked up some junk food. As we walked back toward the car, we noticed the back door was open. A woman dressed like she was one who serviced truck drivers, had one foot in the door. She spoke loud enough for us to hear her ask Preacher if she could help him.

Preacher told her he was a Baptist minister, that he just came from a meeting, and was trying to get some rest. "How old are you, little girl?" he asked. As she removed her foot from the door, she sarcastically replied, "Why should you care?"

Preacher told her he had sisters whom he loved and that she brought back memories. He asked her if she was a Christian. Her attitude changed, she became somber and dropped her head, as she told him she was not. She told him her mother used to drag her to church, but that was some time ago.

He pulled a little copy of the New Testament from his pocket and said, "This little book tells a story of Mary Magdalene. She was a lady of the night until she met Jesus. After her salvation, her name is mentioned in the Bible more than the apostles. Her story is in here to tell the world that it does not matter who you are, where you have been, or what you have done. Jesus loves you, and there is still hope."

He asked her if she would pray with him. She bowed her head and repeated the Sinner's Prayer. "If I were you, little lady," preacher said, "I would go in the shop and call your mother. Tell her you found Jesus, and He has helped you."

As we drove off, Preacher told us we had just witnessed a slice of life. We were tired and the only thing we wanted to do was get home. We were disgruntled that our travel time would be a lot longer, but God had another plan. To accomplish that plan, He gave us a detour.

"I used to wonder," Preacher said, "about what happens to people that are saved and we never see them again. One day I was reading how Jesus told his disciples he would make them fishers of men. I felt God say, 'Dallas, I will take care of that. I have called you to be a fisher of men, you catch them, and I will clean them.'"

Many advertisements feature dramatic before-and-after pictures: balding men who've "regrown" thick hair; a three-hundred-pound woman who is now half her previous size; a teen's face covered in acne until he uses the advertised product. In the after picture, the teen's skin has been treated—and then airbrushed—to perfection. Advertisers use this method because it touches something in us that longs for transformation.

"Therefore, if any man be in Christ, he is a new creation: old things are passed away; behold, all things are become new" (2 Cor. 5:17 KJV).

One of the most dramatic before-and-after stories in the gospels is the transformation of Mary Magdalene. **Before**, she was possessed by seven demons (Mark 16:9). Society considered her unclean and marginalized her both socially and spiritually. **After** Jesus drove the demons out of her, Mary became one of His most devoted followers. She supported Jesus with her financial resources and stuck with Him until the end, present at the cross, the tomb and—joyfully! —at Jesus's resurrection. Encountering Jesus transformed the life of Mary Magdalene, and it is meant to transform lives today.

What is **your** before picture? Who were you, or where would you be today, without Christ? As the song, "Remind Me" says, "To show me where you've brought me from and where I might have been." What is your **after** picture? How has Jesus transformed your life? In what ways is He still working to conform you to His image?

Perhaps you are still in need of an **after** picture. In faith believing, ask forgiveness of your sins. Faith tells me that no matter what lies ahead of me, God is already there.

Chapter 20

TILL WE MEET AGAIN

PREACHER WAS ASKED TO PRESIDE OVER A FUNERAL. His secretary called me and asked if I could sing one song at the service. She told me the name of the funeral home and the date and time.

I arrived early to check the setup. When the preacher came, he said we needed to pray. He told me the funeral was for a six-year-old girl who had died from an infection. "This is going to be rough," he said. He had spoken with the parents, and they could not accept their daughter's death. The mother had told him the father loved the little girl more than life.

The father stayed by the coffin and said he wanted to be there in case she woke up. I had sung for several funerals, but never with this much tension. We stood at the back of the room, waiting for the time to start. I asked if it would be okay to sing from there in the back, a cappella. I sang "Amazing Grace" while preacher walked to the podium. His sermon was about those who God calls before they reach the age of accountability. He said they went immediately to heaven and were free of all pain, held in the arms of Jesus.

Sometimes the sobbing was louder than the talking.

At the end of the service, I walked up for the viewing and sat in the front row in case Preacher needed help. The parents stood by the casket, and it appeared they would not move away. The funeral director placed two chairs beside the casket, and they sat down. Preacher sat down with me, and we waited in silence for a time. Finally, Preacher said, "As I said before, your little girl is in the arms of Jesus. You never have to grieve for her; she is safe, and happy.

"Now, let me ask you a question. Are you a Christian?" Through their sobbing, each gave a slight shake of the head, no. There was a long pause, and then he said, "I am told your greatest desire is to be with your little one. You may think I am hard-hearted when I say this at this difficult time, but I speak in love. Jesus loves you. If you ever want to see and hold your little one in your arms again, you must be saved. Jesus said, '*Except a man be born again, he cannot see the kingdom of God.*' John 3:3

"When that cover is closed, if you have not been born again, you will never see that little one again. Would you give your heart to Jesus this morning? Then you can have the hope of one day seeing Jesus and holding your girl in your arms once again."

They both slid off their chairs to their knees with their elbows on the chair and their faces in their hands. Preacher opened his Bible and read to them the plan of salvation.

> Luke 15:10," *Likewise, I say unto you, there is joy in the presence Of the angels of God over one sinner that repenteth.*"

When they arose, I felt the sobbing had turned into tears of Joy. These situations require the strength of God. While most Christians balk at saying anything in these cases, preacher always felt he might never have another chance to tell of the saving grace of Christ and be held accountable.

That was over fifty years ago, but the memory is as clear in my mind as if it happened yesterday.

Chapter 21

STRANDED

We finished the evening service at a church near Youngstown, Ohio. We were happy for the souls that had given their hearts to God. It was getting late. We had a long day and were eager to get started on the forty-five-minute drive home to rest. The church pastor walked preacher, Charles, Clyde, and I out to our car.

We noticed an older gentleman near us was having automobile problems. He said his car would not start. We tried to assist without success. The pastor walked back to the church to call a service garage for help. (Note: this was BC—before cell-phones.) The man said he was retired, and it seemed like every day since retirement there was a calamity. Preacher said, "Does it seem to you now, as you grow older, that life is short?"

The gentleman hesitated, then said he had listened to the sermon but now had a lot of questions. Preacher said, "The Bible says, *'Life is like a vapor, that appears for a while and then vanishes'* (James 4:14). It also says, *'It is appointed unto men once to die, and after this the judgement'* (Heb. 9:27). It seems almost everyone has a fear of death, but that is not the problem. The problem is after that, and after that is the judgement. The judgement Is where you will spend eternity, Heaven or Hell. The question you must answer is simple, what have you done with my son, Jesus. Has there ever been a time in your life you asked God for forgiveness of your sins?"

The man shook his head, no. Preacher put his hand on his shoulder and said, "Let me tell you something, dad. Yes, life is short, but eternity is forever. You heard me speak about hell tonight. Why not make your eternity forever in Heaven?" Preacher led the gentleman in repeating the Sinner's Prayer, and another name was written down in glory.

The mechanic finally arrived. He checked the car over and said, "Give it another try." It started right up. On the way home, we discussed what happened. No one saw the mechanic do anything except open the hood and look around.

We were wide awake now and discussed what we had witnessed all the way home and passionately believed that God had his hand in everything. He not only controls the universe, but He controls if a car will start or not. We saw two miracles, one the starting of the car and the other the greatest miracle ever performed, and that is saving a lost soul. How He can take a heart filled with sin and wash it white as snow. Isaiah 1:18," *Come now and reason together, saith the Lord: though your sins be as scarlet, they shall be as white as snow; though they be red like crimson, they shall be as wool."*

Chapter 22

THE TRAVELER

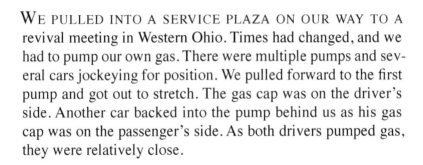

WE PULLED INTO A SERVICE PLAZA ON OUR WAY TO A revival meeting in Western Ohio. Times had changed, and we had to pump our own gas. There were multiple pumps and several cars jockeying for position. We pulled forward to the first pump and got out to stretch. The gas cap was on the driver's side. Another car backed into the pump behind us as his gas cap was on the passenger's side. As both drivers pumped gas, they were relatively close.

The car behind us looked new. The driver was an older gentleman, dressed immaculately. His wife had also stepped out to stretch. Both exhibited an air of sophistication. The man was having trouble getting the gas started. He began letting loose a stream of foul words, cursing the hot weather, the high humidity, and many other things. You could sense he cursed not only when he was angry, but that cursing was a part of his vocabulary.

There were four other cars in the station with women and children. He spoke loud enough that all these people could easily hear him. Preacher took a few steps toward the man and put his hand on his shoulder. He said, "Dad—if you will permit me to call you Dad—do you realize that when you curse and take God's name in vain you are cursing the best friend you will ever have?" Preacher spoke softly. The man asked who he was.

Preacher told him he was a Baptist preacher, headed west to hold a revival meeting. "I listened to your cursing and, thinking perhaps our paths would never cross again, I felt I must talk with you." He told the man it looked like God had been good to him, that God had bestowed him with all this life's goods. He said, "Sir, when you curse, did you ever consider how much the one you cursed loves you?"

The man confessed he had not been raised to speak that way. Preacher pulled the small Bible from his inside pocket and said, *"God's word says, 'If we confess our sins, He is faithful and just to forgive us our sins and to cleanse us from all unrighteousness'"* (1 John 1:9 KJV).

There, with the sound of motors and horns blowing, heads were bowed, and forgiveness asked. The man raised his head and, with tears in his eyes, took his wife's hand and told her how glad he was they made this trip. We got in the car and headed on our way. Preacher said, "You know, if we make this trip without another person being won for Christ, that one man was worth the trip. We know there was a new name written in glory."

This episode recalls how Jesus went through a city, and the Bible said he never passed that way again. How often have we met an individual one time and never saw them again? Will we be held accountable if we do not tell them about Jesus?

Part 4

MESSAGES

Chapter 23

PEANUTS

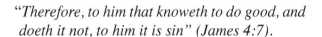

*"Therefore, to him that knoweth to do good, and
doeth it not, to him it is sin" (James 4:7).*

ONE DAY, A FAMILY WAS COMING HOME FROM CHURCH
when Mom turned around in the front seat and asked Johnny in
the back seat what he had learned in Sunday school.

Johnny said, "Oh, we learned all about this guy called Mosey.
He was leading this bunch of people called Isams And they
came to this large body of water. They didn't know what to do
because they were being chased by these Egeys. So, Mosey had
his corps of engineers build a pontoon bridge across the water.
Then all his jeeps and tanks and people crossed to the other
side. The Egeys followed, and when they got to the middle of
the bridge, Mosey picked up his cell phone and called back to
the missile base. They sent up a ballistic missile with an atomic
warhead on it, and it landed smack-dab in the middle of the
bridge. And you know mom, they ain't never been seen since."

His mom said, "Now, Johnny, surely your Sunday school
teacher didn't tell you that."

And Johnny said, "Well, no, not exactly, but if you would have heard the way she told it, you would have never believed it."

There are times we are all guilty of reading or hearing a verse of scripture we do not fully understand, so we put our own interpretation on it. When we do not understand, remember the Bible was written to be believed.

We all remember *Peanuts* with Charlie Brown, Lucy, Snoopy, and the whole gang. Who could forget Lucy intimidating Charlie Brown into kicking the football? Or the specials, like Charlie Brown Christmas.

I remember one *Peanuts* comic strip in particular. There were three panels. In the first one, Marcie is giving her teacher a beautiful vase of flowers picked from the field. The second features her overjoyed teacher, smiling from ear to ear. The caption read, "Thank you, Marcie; You made my day." The third was a picture of Peppermint Patty. It read, "I thought about doing the same thing but just never got around to it."

The question of the day is, "Could you use a vase full of good intentions? How much is a vase full of good intentions worth?"

Let's admit it. We have all had intentions of doing something good but failed to follow through. We may want to make a phone call, check on a relative, write a note of encouragement, or visit a sick friend. Maybe we intended to tell our pastor, teacher, or singer how they blessed us but never got around to it. Christians often have a desire to grow closer to the Lord, but do not get around to reading God's Word or praying. What is it you have been putting off?

A vase full of good intentions never brightened anyone's day. A vase full of good intentions never brought a smile to someone's face. A vase full of good intentions never put a rainbow in someone's dark, stormy day. You may say, "I never know what to say in the moment," but remember, no one will say you talk too much when you're telling them how great they are.

A little girl named Julie went next door to see her neighbor, as she often had, however, the neighbor had recently lost her husband in death. A few days later the neighbor said to Julie's mother, "I was so glad to see Julie. She really made my day." When Julie came home from school, her mother asked her what she had said to the neighbor and Julie answered, "I didn't say anything. I crawled up on her lap, put my arms around her neck, and cried with her."

Blind and deaf Helen Keller said, "The most beautiful things in the world cannot be seen or touched—they must be felt with the heart." Friendship is not the words we say but the loving intentions in our heart.

A man late for his son's ball game leaned over the dugout and asked what the score was. The boy responded, "Eighteen to nothing—we're behind." The man said, "Wow, I guess you're discouraged." The boy said, "Why? We haven't got up to bat yet."

There are no hopeless situations, only people who have grown hopeless about them. That is where we come in, like Barnabas, the encourager, to lend a hand or a kind word. Try to be a rainbow in someone's storm cloud.

The epitaph on a tombstone read, "He lived, he died—who cares?" That is a sad story. I believe an even sadder story would be, "He lived, he died—everybody cared, but no one told him." No matter how good someone is in their art, job, or occupation, they still like to hear words of encouragement. We need to brighten someone's day with a vase full of good actions, not simply good intentions. The best action we can offer is to tell others, "You need Jesus."

"Do not judge each day by the harvest you reap but by the seeds that you plant" (Robert Louis Stevenson).

Some may know Jesus Christ is the only way to Heaven. Perhaps they have heard the message many times. They plan to trust Him someday, but have never gotten around to it. A vase full of good intentions will not bring salvation to anyone.

Years ago, I wrote a song entitled, "Today."

> *Today is the day the day of salvation,*
> *Tomorrow may be too late,*
> *What's your soul's destination*
> *He has said that my spirit*
> *Shall not always strive with man,*
> *Why not open your heart to Him,*
> *And accept Jesus while you can.*

You must believe and repent and ask forgiveness from sins. Just keep in mind as we read the Bible we see where Jesus went through certain cities and never went that way again. Likewise, Jesus may never pass your way again.

> *"For whosoever shall call upon the name of the Lord shall be saved"* (Rom. 10:13 KJV).

If you have never asked forgiveness from sin, you can do that now.

With your heart you could say, *Father, I believe Jesus died on the cross for my sins. I know I am a sinner. Please forgive me of all my sins and save me, for Christ's sake. I will serve you for the rest of my life. Thank you, Lord, for saving my soul.* If you say that with your heart, then according to God's word you have been born again.

What have we learned? That a vase full of good intentions will never brighten anyone's day; a vase full of good intentions will never bring a smile to someone's face; a vase full of good intentions will never put a rainbow in someone's storm cloud. 'However, loving, intentional actions can have a profound effect on the lives of others.'

My prayer is we will endeavor to offer a vase full of good actions to everyone we meet. As they say, "I can't hear what you are saying over what you are doing."

The devil says, "They're all mine."

Jesus responds, *"Over My dead body."*

Chapter 24

THE SERMONS

"PREACHER, DO YOU FEEL YOUR SERMONS ARE DIF-ferent, and is that why so many come to listen?"

"First, it's not about me," he said. "I want my theme to be Jesus, for Jesus is the Bible, starting in Genesis all the way through to the book of Revelation. There is no other gospel.

"My contention is that it does not matter your profession, rich or poor, gender, age, race, or nationality. The hour will come when you need Jesus. I want to talk to them all without reservation, to win the lost whatever the cost. I want people to know my aim in life is to preach Christ. My sermons begin and end with holding up and glorifying Jesus Christ to the world.

"To preach you must believe, turn from your sin, seek God, read your Bible and learn to pray. Some preacher's sermons are ninety percent about the familiar stories in the Old Testament. Others mostly concern themselves with the end of time and Heaven. These can be tremendous sermons. I also preach on these topics. However, I feel the people want to hear about the present. They want to hear what is happening in the world today, and how it will affect them and what they can do.

"Years ago, I was still building tires and attending a local church when I started a radio program with my own money. I began receiving a lot of mail. They wrote wanting me to pray for them and asked a lot of questions. One question was like yours. They said, 'We have a lot of churches in Akron. What makes you think you can start another one, and why would anyone come to listen?' I received some flack when I broadcast my answer.

"I said, 'I sincerely believe there are some good churches in Akron, but I also believe the reason that so many churches do not grow today is that the pastor has become a playboy, sailing, golfing, and bowling instead of calling on his flock concerning their souls. There is never any reward for lost time, and every hour a pastor loses in winning the lost is gone forever.'"

That is when my mind brought forth the picture of Preacher almost every Sunday, strolling up to the microphone with his Bible in one hand and the front page of the Akron Beacon Journal in the other. His messages were fresh and up to date. He would read the words from the paper about last night's happenings or what was to come, and then open God's Word and read almost the same words.

Preacher's desire was to present the gospel with the theory that, "If you put the cookies on the bottom shelf where the kids can reach them, everyone can enjoy."

> *"If I be lifted up from the earth, I will draw all men unto me"* (John 12:32 KJV).

I saw a plaque that read, 'Live in such a way that those who know you, but don't know God, will come to know God, because they know you.'

Chapter 25

THE JOY OF GOD

A MAN LAY IN A HOSPITAL BED SURROUNDED BY HIS family and pastor. The man motioned for a paper and pen. When he finished writing, he handed the note to the pastor and passed away. The pastor stuck the note in his coat pocket without reading it. After the funeral service, they were standing at the gravesite when the pastor put his hand in his pocket and discovered the note. He pulled the note out and announced that since the man always gave encouraging words, he would now read his last thoughts.

The note read, "Pastor, you're standing on my oxygen tube."

This joke only alerts us to the fact that we all are born to die. That time has already been set by God. We do not know that time, therefore, it behooves us to be prepared when the Master calls. If we have been born again, we can say like the apostle Paul, "*O death, where is thy sting? O grave, where is thy victory?*" (1 Corinthians 15: 55)

For the Christian there is joy in knowing, "to *be absent from the body is to be present with the Lord.*" (2 Corinthians 5:8)

Previously, we discussed how important the past is to the future. Now, let us examine how our past and present affect our future. Psychologists recognize the only way you can intellectually make plans for the future is by drawing on your memories of the past. That includes your mistakes as well as the positive choices you have made. The most important influencing factor are the people you meet along the way. Therefore, I am telling my story of the one man who helped guide my future, and in doing so, perhaps encouraged someone else to keep the faith through me.

I am sure you remember the movie, "Back to the Future." When it comes to past ministers who have impressed their name on society, we think of Charles Spurgeon, Billy Sunday, Dwight L. Moody, Billy Graham, and Dallas Billington. They are noted for their large service attendances, but there is something else they all had in common—the desire to see lost souls saved.

Moody said, "I try to preach hell so fervently that the people can feel the blistering heat on the bottom of their feet."

Preacher said, "I want people to know my aim in life is to preach Christ. My messages begin and end with holding up Jesus Christ."

All these messengers of God preached about the Holy Spirit; they preached about sin; they preached about hell. The question for you today is, "When was the last time your pastor preached on these subjects?" Statistics by such agencies as the Barna Group reveal fifty-two percent of ministers across the country admit they do not preach the whole Bible. They do not preach on such topics as same sex marriage, murdering of little babies in the mother's womb, hell, or sin. The reason they give is they are afraid it may offend someone, and they would lose attendance.

Forty-seven percent of millennials say it is wrong to preach the Lord's command given in Mark 16:15-16, *"And He said unto them, go into all the world, and preach the gospel to every creature. He that believeth and is baptized shall be saved, but he that believeth not shall be damned."*

Their stance is, "It is wrong to share one's personal beliefs with someone of a different faith in hopes they will one day share the same faith." In other words, almost half of millennial Christians in North America today in their twenties and thirties believe it is wrong to evangelize someone of a different faith. Millennials wake up and smell the coffee, or should I say, smell the smoke of hell.

Also, sixty-five percent of millennials graduating from Bible seminaries are not sure there is a hell.

Preacher said, "I feel a deep responsibility to go after every man and woman that I meet and win them for Christ."

Would to God all ministers felt the importance. It makes you wonder if this is the beginning of the "great falling away" mentioned in the Bible?

When Jesus said, "go into the world and preach the gospel," can you imagine Peter saying, "You mean those who murdered you?"

"Yes, find the man who spit in my face. Tell him I have a seat in my kingdom just for him if he will believe."

"Master, you mean the man who made the crown of thorns and jammed it on your head?"

"Yes, find him. Tell him I have a crown of glory waiting for him in my kingdom, and it does not have any thorns. Will you believe?"

"But Master, you mean the one who struck you with the reed?"

"Yes, find him and tell him I have a scepter for him to hold if he will accept salvation."

"Lord, you can't mean the soldier who drove the spear into your side?"

"Yes, seek him out, tell him there is a nearer way to my heart. Peter, tell them it doesn't matter your profession, rich or poor, gender, age, race, or nationality. They need Jesus."

> *"For I am the way. the truth, and the life. No one comes to the father except through me"* (John14:6 KJV).

Think about it—we have a large segment of those who say they are Christians telling God He is wrong. Their ideals are 180 degrees diametrically opposed to what God commands. It seems to me we heard this story before in the Garden of Eden. *"And the serpent said unto the woman, Ye shall not surely die"* (Gen. 3:4 KJV).

This is Satan's chief subtlety, to cause us to fear and question God. We should not question God but rather question anyone who questions God. We not only need to compare the words of others to God's word; we also need to question their music. Check the internet regarding Bethel and Hillsong music.

As we see how this world turns, we need to seek God's leadership in both our daily lives and in our Christian service and represent God to others. Then we will see our faith grow. In conclusion, let us remember, "God Isn't Dead." James tells us, *"My brethren, count it all joy when ye fall into divers' temptations, knowing this, that the trying of your faith worketh patience"* (James 1:2-3 KJV).

"for the joy of the Lord is your strength" (Neh. 8:10). This verse could be interpreted to read: No Joy, No Strength. The theme of joy is what the world needs now more than ever. Just as with all our trials, tribulations and world conditions we felt it could not get worse, along comes the coronavirus 19. If you need something to rejoice about, just remember ever since time began, in the garden, the temple, the cross, the church; this God who made everything wants to dwell with us. David questioned why God was even mindful of him.

Some people have those in their own household that doesn't want them to be there. Yet God is moving heaven and earth just so He can be with us. That should bring Joy to your heart. By accepting His Son, Jesus Christ, He has filled us with all the power we will ever need to confront this world and wants to someday crown us with a crown of victory. God is saying if we are lacking strength it is because we are lacking joy. No joy, no strength.

If there is anything this world needs to combat this virus, sorrow, and fear going around is a good old fashion dose of the joy of the Lord. God wants us to rejoice and be glad, because the price has already been paid for our sins, the victory is ours, death has been conquered, the chains of sin has been broken, our burdens have been lifted, we have been filled with his power, and God says again rejoice.

No Joy, No strength. So, if we want strength and power in our lives, first think how we were condemned to die for our sins and Jesus died on the cross to save us. That alone should cause us to rejoice. Give thanks and be filled with joy.

Secondly, we experience the joy of the Lord through prayer.

Thirdly, the reading of God's word brings joy. We need to go to the fountain where that joy is found. To immerse ourselves in God's word. To drink deeply of it and savor the fellowship with God.

Fourthly, joy through the power of the Holy Spirit. When the Spirit opens our eyes, we truly are filled with the overwhelming joy of the Lord. God is love, God is joy, and God the Father and God the Son and God the holy Spirit are one. Therefore, if we are filled with the Holy Spirit, we have joy unspeakable that we can tap into continuously.

My prayer is that our hearts will be filled with joy, and that our joy will show forth so others can see Christ living in us, even if we do not tell them.

"And when these things begin to come to pass, look up, lift up your heads, for your redemption draweth nigh" (Luke 21:28 KJV).

While we wait for the Lord's return, think of Rev. Dallas F. Billington's motto, "Win the Lost at Any Cost." Amen.

ACKNOWLEDGEMENTS

I WOULD LIKE TO THANK LINDA LONSDORF FOR helping to guide me through the writing of this book. It has been quite a process, and I have valued her help and unwavering support.

Thanks to Dr. Charles F. Billington, son of Dr. Dallas F. Billington, who took over the helm of the church at his father's death and continued to lead the congregation through tumultuous times.

Special thanks to Charles F. Billington Jr. and Rev. Dallas R. Billington, sons of Dr. Charles Billington, for their assistance in materials acquisition.

Many thanks to Tom Secrest, Graphic Designer, for putting together an outstanding binder.

GOD IS REAL

T<small>HE MOST IMPORTANT BOOK IN MY LIBRARY IS THE</small> Bible. The #2 book in my library is entitled, God Is Real. It was written in 1962 by my grandpa, Dallas F. Billington. Like the Bible, it too has become a "light unto my feet." If Grandpa were to write another book today, I think it could be entitled, "God is Still Real," or "On the Other Side of the Pulpit."

Reverend Dallas R. Billington, pastor City Church AC

PREAMBLE

BEHIND EVERY GREAT MAN IS A GREAT WOMAN. THIS idiom also applies to great ministers. Here is another idiom: Before every great preacher is a soloist.

Before Dwight Moody, there was Ira Sankey. Before Billy Graham, there was George Beverly Shea. Before Dr. Dallas Billington, there was Neal Kendall.

This book is not about me. It's about a country preacher, Dallas F. Billington, who stood behind the pulpit and described the horrors of hell and told his flock the only way to escape hell was to accept Christ.

I wrote this book to show it is possible for a man of God to uphold his Christian standards. Dr. Billington carried the same message, whether he was out of the pulpit living his daily life through this sinful world, or behind the pulpit preaching the word of God.

I caught glimpses of those occasions as I traveled with him to sing at evangelistic meetings and various church and senior center dedications. Preacher's theme was, "Win the Lost at any Cost," whether behind the pulpit or on the other side.

(Please note the "PREAMBLE "is about the book and can be called anything AND "ABOUT THE AUTHOR" BOTH go on the back of the binder)

ABOUT THE AUTHOR

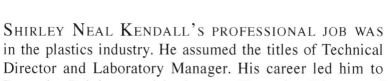

SHIRLEY NEAL KENDALL'S PROFESSIONAL JOB WAS in the plastics industry. He assumed the titles of Technical Director and Laboratory Manager. His career led him to Brussels, Belgium, and he became Executive Director of European Operations. He also served as an expert plastics witness in court proceedings.

His company sent him to Belgium to build two plastic processing plants. However, it became clear that God sent him there to build a church. It was estimated that 25,000 English-speaking people resided in Brussels and did not have a church home because the language in the churches was French or Flemish.

An English-speaking church was established, and Neal taught the adult Bible class until they hired two full time Baptist ministers.

Neal taught Bible classes in Brussels, in Anniston, Alabama, and at the Akron Baptist Temple. His first love was quartet singing and close harmony. He was also a featured soloist at the Akron Baptist Temple.

When the founder and pastor of the temple, Dallas Billington, traveled to minister at other churches, church dedications, senior home meetings, or political speeches, Neal went with him to sing and lead the music.

He has been a member of several gospel quartets through the years and continues to perform. Preacher was so much a part of Neal's early life, he said when he retired, he wanted to tell others of his pastor's unwavering Christian standards.

Neal has been blessed with three sons, Kevin, Kent, and Kurt. Three daughters in law, Mayra, Megan, and Mary. Six grandchildren, Kristopher, Gia, Grace, Kate, Ariana and Logan.

CPSIA information can be obtained
at www.ICGtesting.com
Printed in the USA
BVHW090849130121
597694BV00007B/14

9 781662 805684